# Signs Round
# a Dead Body

for my father
and
with the memory of my grandmother,
Mabel Ellinor Rees-Jones (1903-1994)

# Signs Round
# a Dead Body

# Deryn Rees-Jones

seren

**seren** is the book imprint of
Poetry Wales Press Ltd
2 Wyndham Street, Bridgend, Wales, CF31 1EF

A CIP record for this title is available
from the British Library

ISBN 1-85411-241-4

*The publisher works with the financial support of the*
*Arts Council of Wales*

Cover image: 'Portrait of the late Mrs Partridge'
by Leonora Carrington, by permission of the
Edward James Foundation, Chichester

Printed in Palatino
by WBC Book Manufacturers, Bridgend

# CONTENTS

## I

## II

## III

## IV

*O living always — always dying!*
*O the burials of me...!*
Walt Whitman

# I

# Signs Round a Dead Body

Some day, by chance, you'll find that you're the first
To find the body of a man:

As you walk one evening in an unknown wood,
Or stroll along a secret beach — drunk or asleep? — or worse
Enter a long familiar room
Which has a silent staring body
At its corner or its end.

Remember, then, that it's your duty to remember:
How the hand lay on the ground precisely, how the neck
Was placed, despairingly, the line of vertebrae,
A turn of ankle or a turn of head. If you've no camera
You must note exactly how his soft dark hair's
Rained green with light or leaves.
Note how each toe is unresponsive when it's tickled,
By opening door, by rabbit, or a sleepy tide; the way that
Pine cones, or novellas have been thoughtlessly
Strewn round him — silent as himself, like meteors, unopened gifts,
Like huge forgotten shells.

And you must check whether the ground or floor's disturbed or
Trampled down, whether the leafy carpet's crumpled,
Scarred with ash, or trailed with blood.

Remember it's your duty to examine and write down
The smallest sign which may be vitally important.
Use your eyes! Be vigilant! Let nothing
Be too small! And when you've finished, and you must return,

Open the newspaper you found at some inconsequential place.
Sit for some time, and read perhaps. Take three deep breaths.
If it is possible, drink tea. After a while,
follow the murmuring voices and the faceless snores
That are the other men,
Whose sounds that strangely amplify at night
Appear from nowhere like a thread.

# Horoscopes

*for Rachel and Nicola*

*Libra*, your horoscope predicts
A tall dark man, a hairy dog. I say
He'll come by parachute on May the 8th,
Striding across your neat suburban lawn,
Dragging his harness and his silks
Before he scoops you magically with
Just one freckled arm and carries you
Away. A part of just-made history. The dog?
The hairy dog? Well, that's there too.
You *love* the dog. Your face, to say the least,
Reads sceptical. *Taurus*. We'll say no more.
The bull. This week you are advised *Get tough*
*But show your man you're vulnerable*. Destiny
Speaks secret meetings in a health food store.
For *Gemini* (that's me) true love must wait
Till Tuesday. The stars spell out an S, a
Radio request. Your marriage chart is hot.
There is no better fate. For all you men out there
Remember me? Oh, how we laugh, berate ourselves,
Dance with the clammy ghosts of chance.
We're scared by love, and scared by the lack of it,
That's true, asking like children, now,
Unable to imagine it again. Feeling too old for guesses,
Suppositions, doubts. Anticipating touch and sudden
Reckless kisses: *Who will it be, when will it be,*
*Where will it be, and how?*

# The One That Got Away

In the Midleton factory
Where you worked for three summers
You fell for a woman
You swore you would marry
If only for the sake
Of the tale you could tell
Years later,
About the day when you met:
This doe-eyed, wide-hipped,
Inspectress of Peas, who,

Testing for sweetness, consistency,
Size — this will kill you, you said —
With the *Pea Tenderometer*,
You made jump from her skin
(Sweet Jesus, this your only sin:
To lean across her gently,
Nibble at the darted cotton apron
Covering her breasts
And whisper how you wanted her....)
And who, in fear, surprise,

Punched a perfect, pea-shaped hole
Straight through your thumb.
These days, when you hold your hand
Up to the light, squint through yourself
Like a painter, with one eye open
And one eye closed
At all the aching sky,
And start on this story
With a squeeze and a smile,
I'm still not sure.

*The one that got away?*
The pea-shaped flesh?
The pear-shaped girl?

# The Fish

*"Rainbow, rainbow, rainbow!"*

E.B.

I go to sleep with the taste of you, and this is not the first time

for you are too much with me. And these are your hands,
in the darkness. This is the rough shape of
your face, only. Your hair, your ear, your thigh.
      And then, out of nowhere, your tongue like a hot little fish
a blue fish, glinting electrics,
a fish accustomed to basking, I suppose,
in the clear hot waters of some tropical isle.
Not an ordinary fish, not a fish I could haul from the waters,
                    or not easily.
Not a fish accustomed to travelling in solitude,
but one used to a rainbow accompaniment,
one used to the sea's depths, and her sulky harbourings.
One used to the rockpools and the undertow, the colour of
                    the sands.
And, how suddenly you swam into me!
      And was it your mouth, or the memory of your mouth?
Or was it a fish? Whatever it was, it was there.
There in the bloodstream, bruising artery, vein,
as it swam,
heading, no doubt, for the heart.
Then you stopped it,
         for you knew it would have killed me,
and it basked in the blue pools of my elbow, where you
stroked it for a while;
then you asked it to dart, from my hips up my spine,
you asked it to wander to the tilt of my breastbone
where tickled, like a salmon, it leapt
      it leapt;
you asked it to journey from my shoulder to my neck, to that
                  soft place
behind my ears
where you solemnly forbade it, asked it instead to
rest for a while, and then turn back,

saying *Fish, fish, my brilliant fish*
        and something I can't
remember now

on the furthermost tip of my tongue, like a dream.

# Sheep Piece

## (i) The couple

Remember the photo the sheep took of us?
My face made tentative and ugly in the sun,

and you in the shirt that would've matched your eyes,
except that you were (humbly?)

looking at the ground?
We couldn't understand a word she said,

but somehow, as it came about, there was no need
for spoken promises or speeches, no need

for *Smile, please!* or a grudging
teeth-clenched *Cheese!* In a sheepish way

we looked and locked so perfectly together —
my flowing bright blue skirt hitched up,

my shoelaces, my plaited hair, undone.
And I really can't remember why we got down on our knees

except we weren't quite able to believe
— who could — in such a sudden, perfect

kind of love, or even in ourselves,
that summer, let alone the sheep,

the coloured Polaroid emerging
and all the attendant angels fussing round.

## (ii) The sheep

As if four legs were an eternal condemnation
to a horizontal life! As if they'd never seen
a sheep before, gone vertical! They thought
I was a god, the tightened curls of my golden coat
shining and radiant. Not a rare breed,
badger-faced or speckled, just a local,
newly-washed and happy, afro-combed.
And yet it was as if I was about
to steal their souls, the way they looked at me,
so innocent, like children
as they prayed there on the stubbly
sheep-chewed ground. And then, another thing,
they were amazed I shared a language with them,
rated their technologies, could wield a Kodak
good as any other sheep. They blinked and
shuffled, finding I was eloquent, a little bossy,
charming, perspicacious, sometimes rude. But
proud of sheep-heritage, glad to be ruminant
and beardless, progressive, self-controlled....

(Okay, I was an amateur, but it was just
that moment that I wanted:
them making sheep's eyes
as the sun, glowing behind them,
slipped gently through the trees.)

## (iii) The photograph

Funny how it starts. With an itch
when it's least expected. How it spreads
like a blush would, on a body of velvet,
a spreading soft discordance
edging slowly through the spectrum
until you are a shiny hard oasis
sucking all the colours in.
You have to make yourself remember
how you always start from scratch
before your features decompose
into dimensions, all
your plain, white surface areas confused.
You have to tell yourself
it's only transient, until
like chameleon, you find
you're doing it again, with someone,
something else. Being a woman, now,
and smaller than she'd thought,
and younger, a man, quite boyish
and wild-haired. That's when you start to hurt,
feeling the strain of everything contained,
each particle, each colour. You're not
yourself, the photographic paper or
the thing you photographed:
the lovers or the landscape.
Not the moment when you stole them either,
all that bemusement and contentment,
all those colours, all that joy,
ventriloquised imperfectly, so perfectly:
flesh-coloured flesh. The girl, the boy.

# Making Out

Now it was airports that she needed —
to sit there going nowhere
counting aeroplanes like sheep,

with Concorde like an archaeopteryx or angel,
and Egypt, Russia, the Azores and Lithuania
spinning in her head. She'd sit there

writing letters that she knew she wouldn't send,
telling him about the dull red moon, the way
the landscape then, so pale, unreal,

the fishermen, the midnight seas,
had been tattooed like hieroglyphs
in blues and golds

deep into her skin. It was his hands, I think,
she could imagine best,
travelling across her. But she thought about the way

he'd kiss her, too, the way she'd smile, nod yes
to his demolishing her. The way he'd start
to reassemble, slowly, in the rented bed

her mouth, her throat, her shoulders, breasts,
her knees, her arms, her thighs,
her calves, and love etc.

# From His Coy Mistress

Some days I think I will become a nun,
book in a convent miles away,
cut off my hair, and dress in black
wanting to purge myself of men.

I'd kneel and pray and chant a lot,
lie in a narrow bed,
devising titles of unwritten books:
*A Semiotics of Flirtation. Love:*
*Some Concepts of the Verb "To Sin."*

One thing's for sure. By wanting you,
I'm not the woman that I think I am.
I cannot eat or sleep at all,
just think about your lovely mouth

the eerie moonlight and the Northern seas.
And hope my body's still the temple
that you'd come upon, by chance,
to excavate, a hundred years from now,

burn incense in, and dance and sing,
oh, yes and weeping, worship in.

# An Indian Summer

Sometimes it's as if we're lost,
A place on a map that no one can find.
And I have to invent us, over and over,
Give us names that we smile at:
*Nova Nostalgia, Valentine Corner, Lost Love's Grove.*
O my soft and freckled river!
I'm the Edwardian lady in an unmanned boat,
Lying on cushions, with the sun on her face,
Lazily trailing one ungloved hand.

# What It's Like To Be Alive

*after Django Bates*

I remember the nights, and the sounds of the nights,
and the moon, and the clouds, then the clear sky

and the stars and angels on the Rye,
and I remember the way we knelt on the bed, how the bedclothes

were a tide, and the sunlight was a tide, and how everything
                                                    pulled,
and I remember the trains, leaving and arriving,
and I remember the tears, your tears, and my tears

and how we were children, not lovers,
how the angels cried,

and I remember your face and you coming in my hands,
and the clouds, and the stars, and how, for a moment,
with our eyes tight closed how the planets lurched

and the angels smiled,
and I remember how I did not know if this was grief or love,

this hot pool,
and the sounds,
and then nothing.

A watermark held up to the light.
A boat rowed off the edge of the world.

II

# Songs of Despair

*Emerge tu recuerdo de la noche en que estoy.*
*El rio anuda al mar su lamento obstinado.*

*Abandonado como los muelles en el alba,*
*Es la hora de partir, oh abandonado.*

Neruda, 'Song of Despair'

\*

If I made a snow man to remember you,
A sharp-edged ghost, a little god, to better understand you,
If I gave it eyes, a nose, a small set mouth,

If I smiled, and flirted, licked its modelled ear,
Or its icy cheek till my tongue was a flame
Would it come to life,

Its moulded shoulders and its wooden limbs?
Would its frozen heart
Grant me a wish?

Would it dissolve in a flurry as the winds blew over it?
Would it melt
So that matter transformed

So that water,
A muddied pool,
Would be all that was left

So that,
As I knelt,
I could raise you

As if from the dead
To my dried & emptied mouth
*And would the earth still be frozen?*

Frozen.
My footprints in the white fields of Tartarus,
Crows-feet, laughter, feathers-in-the-snow.

23

*

I have sent you away.
I have sent you to where sky meets sea
To the silence         where the sea

Imagines itself;

To the sky,
            Which overcomes us
Being itself and nothing,
                        Simply.

Without purpose, with derision, I have sent you away.
I have sent you drunken, into the dark,
Weighed down with weightlessness.

I have sent you, like an angel fallen from the heavens.
I have wished you lonely, hated and bemused.
I have sent you drunken, into the dark.
I have sent you hatred like a glowing wreath.

I have sent you bitterly, into the dark.
It's there, love, only,
                    That you'll meet me.

*

I said
Make me unfaithful as I sleep
Make me unfaithful waking me from sleep
I said let me give you this thing, I said

Furnish me

With this small hard thing

*Bring me oranges, pomegranates, starfruit.*
*Bring me mangoes, kumquats, pears.*

And make me discover you
                              As you do.

    And how could I blame you for that?
Or my own stink in that stinking room,
With flowers strewn on that hard square bed &
Amethysts in my ears.

*

When I found you, or, as the story goes,
When you found me,

When you took my hand and walked beside the sea,
Or refused to take my hand as we wandered through the hills,

Or when, undressed, I was too scared to face you,
Or when you looked askance at me, and didn't smile,

I did not know if it was love,
Or if love itself was a cure or a disease —

That thing we cannot really name, or see,
Know only symptoms of.

*

So I raised you from the dead.
So I washed you, licked your armpits, the soles of your feet,
                                        untangled
The spidery lines of your matted hair,
Picked the leaves and insects from your well-shaped limbs,
Blew life into your mouth
And sang to you.
So I suckled, promised, fed and enfolded you.
So I hated, loved, scorned even myself,
Was tenderness, a body to you.

And the world was ours,
For you were risen from the dead.

And when you had loved enough,
When you had loved me till love was not even enough;
When you had tied, hurt, salvaged me.
When you had shaved off every hair on your body, as a gift.
When you had carved your name, a scar
                          On my forearm,

I sent you
Back to the dead.

Kicked the soft earth in your sweet mouth,
And left you to the dogs, the emptiness, the hillside
Of your own self

Which even now, in its horror, surprises me.

*

So maybe I will say that I am lost —
That my heart is lost, or that I've lost my heart;
And ghosts, like the memory of water,
Cannot be dissuaded,
            Surface from the newly fallen snow.

So maybe I will say,
Squatting against the coolness of a wall,
Or sleeping on a boat, a transatlantic plane,
That there is nothing left for me to do.

This loving has become a life.

And this is the process of staying alive,
Knowing that you will not come.

*

When I say that your shoulders are an ox's, strong and unlovely,
When I say that your belly and its deeply-set umbilicus
                                 Mean nothing,
When I say that the pits of your eyes beneath their brows, myopic,
                                 Are uncared for,
When I say that the roughness of your cheek,
The unseemly length between nose and lip,
That your elliptical smile,
Or that the noises that you make in sleep,
Your farts, grumbles, dream-debris,
Remind me of a dog,
Or that the tilt of your head, or the crossing of your leg,
Your bearing, in fact
Simply is not beautiful

It is the same as when I take the oath to testify
*I do not love you*

It's the same as when I promise faithfully
That every word I've ever said is true.

29

*

Tonight the trees are heavy with snow,
So remote, and yet so touchable.
I could stand here forever, I suppose,
Watching the street in the streetlight
Stiffen like a corpse, a freshly laundered uniform.

And I could bring you words,
But my lips are frozen, and my tongue is numb.
I could bring you a coffin to bury the words.
I could bring an assemblage of bones —
Hair, particle, living matter —
To question the lack in me, in love.
I could bring the pain between men and women.

I could bring the cold air and the subway and the river;
All the city's sounds.
I could bring you love in a glass of water,
In a touch, in a word.
I could bring you everything, except delight

To blow you open.
I could not bring the blizzard or the storm.

Only myself, only love,
My own taste, my own smell,

Your mouth as my own
As I lean into you

Mingling the startled syntax of our clothes.

*

When you undress me, and you will —
In ten years, or in twenty,

And my greyed hair blows heavily across your shoulders
                                                    like a sail,
When I am the spring tide, and neaps,
                            The high tide about you,
When I'm like a boom, switching in the breeze,
Or, lolling against you, that lone forgotten oar;
When you come to know again my mast, my helm, my
                                            creaking decks,
When you relearn the names
                    By which to call me:
Know me port, fo'c'sle, starboard, bow and stern,

And I am the boat
            In which you sail home to greet me,

Remember me as I was
And the first time
We set out to sea; and see

Now thé scar on my breast
A starry bullet

Where, as I leapt and soared,
With foam in my hair on that tiny raft,

Thoughtlessly as a smile,
An illegible glance,

You looked up, crowing,
                Shot me

III

# Song for Winter

These days, even love is terrible,
Like a plane, taking off inside the heart.
And now there's nowhere left to go.
For you've brought me to the edges of hell
With your soft ways and your gardener's hands;
You, who'd turn your hand, your eye, to anything,
Filling the house with the smell of bread and roasting lamb,
Bringing in wood for the fire from the yard
As if it were a task of love, or something to be guilty of....
And if I cried out in the night, if you cried too,
To the buildings and the lightless houses,
To trucks, to retail parks, to helicopters, taxis,
The digital, the car alarms, who is there to answer?
Who amidst the landscape that I almost recognise,
The rest homes and the hospitals, the pubs,
The restaurants, the neoned clubs, the bric-à-brac
Of roof and trees, a mutilated statue in the park,
Who laughing, who retching, who weeping,
Who is there to tell how sorrow puts a name to sorrow —
With language or the body? T.V., the radio,
The little gods of noise? For we carry love
Like a kind of pain: desire like terror,
A sticklebacked wave.... And who, looking down,
Would offer more than this, a shrug, a look of pity, or a smile?
Who, seeing us now, our gaze upturned, the knowing stars
Like a litter of rice, confetti of fractured bone, of broken glass,
Could pluck us, unhurt from the universe,
Rechart the stars, make everything strange?
What's more, who'd even ask, or have the right to ask,
Why nothing comes of nothing, still?
I play back voices on the ansaphone, a prayer.

*Tree-twist    feather    tangle-hair.*

35

# Song for the Absence of Her Lover's Voice

(i)

A bright day, that might be brighter with you here.

I think about the way that time can fill itself,
How space is dark and replicates until it makes me hurt,
How words, making themselves from nothing, too,
Are all this distance lets us share.

Your presence, meanwhile, like a rhyme, can take me to a
                              corner quietly by the hands

And,
So quietly, my love, so beautifully,
Knows just the way to keep me there.


(ii)

When in our March, our April and our June
We saw a bird, an animal,
That no one knew the name of
We were quiet. The winter came and disappeared too soon.

This silence I remember now. Also the gaps, the breath,
My mouth, the noises that I make.

How after seven days without you I am lost.

On the telephone, a hundred miles away, you tell me all
                                            of this.
Quite unashamed, I steal your poem like I'd steal a kiss.

# Songs for the Weather

## (i) Modal Auxiliaries

I make a fine, bright trail of myself:
You want me, you want me not.

I'm like a flower to pull the petals off.
*I can't, I mustn't, Don't.*

*You are so close I don't know what I'm doing,*
You kill me with the colours in your eyes.

The morning is a red sky. Thunder.
Rainclouds gather overhead.

## (ii) A Day at the Beach

We call this a friendship of beaches:
Ducks and drakes at the waterside,
Your cricketer's arm
Threading the sea with necklaces of stones.

A flock of birds fly eastwards.

I bury myself up to my neck
So only my face can catch
The beady sun, in flames
Of purple-yellow sand.

Later you offer me apples, which I take —
A strange dismembered burning head
Two eyes, a nose, my small pink mouth.

And the starkness of the brilliant green
Tasting the salt on your long fingers,
Crisp bite by gorgeous bite.

## (iii) Cirrus, Cumulus, Stratus, Nimbus

Now only the sky seems simple,
A supple, sleeping snoring blue,
A place I'd like to visit for a while
Where I'd forget my self,
The date, the time, my keys, my head

Subsumed in clouds,
With you entirely dressed in love, in nothing
But the weather.


## (iv) A Kind of Dance

Your light body's like a bird's:
It might be full of air, and nothing else,
Not blood, bone, muscle, hair,
And water, semen, skin.
Now I'm an ocean of guesses,
Losing myself and finding you, lost.
We leap from seaside rock to rock,
Roughly take heart,
Then rock and rock and rock for hours
*Rainstorms, hailstones, avalanche!*
What are the movements that bring us close?


## (v) Listening for the Sea

Sleeping for the first time in the same bed
I press my ear against you
As if you were some large pink fragile shell.
*Speak to me, speak to me, speak to me, speak.*
The quiet becomes itself. We've said it all.
Today we must have walked for miles
Skirting the endless crumbling coast.
I don't know what it is I want to hear.
Pine cones open, seaweeds moisten.
And then your body whispers like the tide

And comes and comes and comes and comes,
Then slowly moves away.


## (vi) A Camera Obscura

Asked for a metaphor for our goodbye
I do of course, refuse,
Needing at least a shifting shore,
You do of course, insist,
Rifling through language for images
Like magic mirrors, periscopes,
A camera obscura for the heart.

Remember the creature we saw in the dunes
So soft and strange,
The one we didn't recognise, the one we couldn't name?
You tell me there are words for everything.
But where are the books that tell you the words — the
                                              special ones
We never hear? For things we see from trains, for
Building parts, for colours
For movements in the stratosphere, ways of hurting,
Things that grow.


## (vii) I am / just is

Now everything's itself, and not itself,
A flower, a tree, a rock, a cloud.
I touch what I name, name what I touch, the rest
Remains intransitive, just is. So I cry
Remember how you thought the other guests
Would think that you were murdering me in bed;
So I touch — thigh, chest, penis, arm,
So I leave,
Feel the sun on my body, the brightness of rain.
Then I cry, make laughter, am, love.

# Song in Praise of Running by the Sea

*innumerable corazon del viento*
*latiendo sobre nuestro silencio enamorado*
                        Neruda, *Twenty Love Poems*

If this is anything it's love,
The body's faith that can allow itself
To put one foot before another as it's learnt,
And then to cartwheel, holler, wave, shake, spin.
You are a breath, a prayer, the sun
On a moving limb, the shift
Of moving nothing into change,
The dull excitement of the muscle as it warms
And then the great surprise
Of everything that's lifting,
The way you have become yourself
The whole anatomy of speed.
            I run as if to capture it,
The taste of sand, the sweat,
A sense of something simple
Being made strange. It is a
Reassurance, too, that for a moment
It might last forever....
This is the way to know the heart.
A warm breeze and the whole world
Feathering with salt the skin.

# Song in Praise of the Art of Flight

*"I say, Peter, can you really fly?"*
*Instead of troubling to answer, Peter flew around the room taking*
*in the mantelpiece on the way.*
*"How topping", said John and Michael.*
*"How sweet", cried Wendy.*
*"Yes, I'm sweet, oh, I am sweet", said Peter, forgetting his manners again.*
        — J.M. Barrie, *Peter Pan and Wendy*

For so long now I've asked you to explain,
Poured over textbooks, manuals, encyclopaedias,
Thought carefully about propulsion, lift,
The tilt of heel, the point of toe,
The angle of the shoulders to the heavens,
The line of neck, the wriggle of the shoulders and the flex
                              of spine,

The way the body follows thoughts:
A push against the flow of air
Letting oneself go with the drift
For miles, then firmly, slowly, entering the world again
With a gasp of letting go...
And now I know the way it must be done,
A face upturned in ecstasy
Like an angel or a comet with your streaming hair;
And a cry, stepping out of time,
Where trust is an absence of thought,
And silence.

Your heart an elevator shaft
                       You just fell through.

# Song for Rain

I want the rain to be in everything,
not a season or an afternoon, but rain in everything:
a clean blue repetitious life.

I want it in fires, gorse fires by the sea, candles that we love by;
when you are drunk, fearful, I want it in dreams;
in feathers, small stones, whole forests of green;
I want it there in the night, when you shout and sweat,
when nothing will comfort you;

when I take your arm,
when I shake my head with sheer joy like a dog,
and the silence is sudden, beautiful, forgiving

I want the rain to be terrible
in my eyes, in my hair.

And I want it in rivers, in stars, its sound, very simply,
familiar among the leaves and rattling the windows
together when we wake.

I want it in wars and the memory of wars,
in pity and fear. Your taut body pushing at mine.

I want it, and you, and the rain, not her

writing herself all over your face.

# Song for the End of Summer

If love was a colour then today
it is a thin and painful blue;
and if it was a place
it's here: the way the sky
has somehow disappeared
into itself, the way the sea runs up
the pebbled shore
and then recedes
and trees begin to do
their many autumn things,
throwing their colours —
yellows, cheerful reds —
so thoughtlessly away.
Holed up inside this
rattling empty house
it's strange
that listening to music,
picking up a half-read book,
makes every corner of the room
now somehow even emptier.
*I love you. You are everywhere.*
There's nothing left to say.

# Song to Noise

I call on you in all your forms.
I call on your crotchets, breves and semibreves, your quavers,
                                                semiquavers.
I call on your laughter and your shouts,
Your stereos, your hand-wound gramophones,
I call on car exhausts, low flying aeroplanes,
On ghetto blasters, walkmans, telephones, on mobile phones, on
                                                fax machines.
I call on your choirs and choristers, your arguments, your cries.
I call on foghorns, shattered glass, your digital alarms,
The caterwaul of traffic on the motorway,
Eartrumpets, typewriters, violins and hearing aids.
I call on you in the whisper of the dying,
In the rush and creak of water in the wainscot pipes.
I call on your lawnmowers, vacuum cleaners,
Your ill-tuned radios, your television sets.
I call on the wetness of fingers circling a glass.
I heap noise on the altar of noise
A bundle of rag and bone cries.
And I call on you and your gongs and cymbals
In all your ragged might
To beat your wings against the silence of death
For love, or what stands for love,
Or life.

IV

# Midnight Beach at Sizewell B

How ordinary it is,
like a shoebox, or a series of shoeboxes,
as if you could assemble it yourself,
make the dome complete, for instance, in a trice,
splitting two straight lines in half
then bending them
till they become two softly touching arcs,
made pale and oddly solid,
silvered in a moment,
a gasp of breath on glass.
Yet still it would be nothing more than ordinary —
in fact it's this you can accept it for —
the line of cars, the lights, its gently low-key whirr,
the men and women on their shift
now laughing, muttering, perhaps, while
diligently clocking on; one tiny, smoking chimney
straying in the starless sky
as if all human error, pain
was quietly taken care of, here —
bundled up, smoothed out, and trimmed;
catapulted centuries away.

# A Brief Inventory of Facts About Snow

*for Mossy*

For months now, I've dreamed of nothing but snow,
How the six-sided crystals which descend on us *ex machina*
Make an underworld of everything
So that waking in the warmth of orange,
Staring through the window at the whitened skies,
I want to go no further, want to fall back, simply,
In a drift of sleep, naming its colours, inconsistencies.
I want to ask the whole world what it makes of snow —
Snow yellowed or purpled, snow trampled, or pristine,
How we remember or remember we've imagined it,
Or when we think we first encountered it
Snow mounting on snow....

     From Scotland, Sally laughs that Andrew,
Feverish, with 'flu, now dreams of going to work on skis.
And I imagine this tall man and the empty bed
As if he'd jumped from the window there and then
Leaving a trail of parallel lines,
His white sheets like a rush of wings,
His hair like a halo as it streams
Gold on white on blue....

     And Julia imagines mountains in a children's book —
Snow like chocolate sauce on white ice cream,
A monochrome version in reverse, while Michael
Shows me exactly how
To save my life in case of avalanche
Launching me upwards through the cold
Swimming a vertical length of snow.

     Alison, telling me to be happy, adds, in passing,
How Breughel, dissatisfied with images
Of families, workers, friends
Going about their daily business in the heat
Repainted canvases to make them winter
Painting the joy of nothing into summer
As if, with snow itself,
He could, by trapping air between the flakes,
Now insulate the heat between the years

Making plants survive, or people even,
Making absence itself
                    Complete;
And I remember April, fifteen years ago,
How Nicola swung on the blossom tree
Making the whole world blush,
How this, in its gentleness, in its surprise,
Was somehow, too, a vision of snow.
        And Moss writes last,
Smiling his way through careful inks,
To tell me the tale of a William Bentley,
Born Jericho, Vermont, and how he spent
His whole life taking photographs of snow,
Proving, beneath the microscope, each flake
As asymmetrical as women's breasts,
No two the same but soft, amorphous, beautiful....
        And all these words become a kind of rhapsody
On the way that snow transforms itself
As I curl up, daydreaming, my knees pulled to my chest,
Falling asleep with an unread book
Thinking, yes, yes, I have to agree,


        *That's the glory*
            *That's the wonder of snow.*

# Snow Song

All summer I've waited,
Weaving this cloth of burrs and nettles
Till my hands
Prickle and blister
Like bubbles of oxygen
Trapped under glass.

Then suddenly the snow:
Snow being born of itself,
Snow feathering your cheeks, lashes, lips,
Snow, being more than itself,
The colour of nothing.
Snow like the wings of a long-necked bird....

And I call you, whispering.
*A few days is all we have.*

# Calcium

Because I love the very bones of you,
and you are somehow rooted in my bone,
I'll tell you of the seven years

by which the skeleton renews itself,
so that we have the chance to be
a person, now and then, who's

something other than ourselves;
and how the body, if deficient,
will bleed the calcium it needs —

for heart, for liver, spleen —
from bone, which incidentally,
I might add, is not the thorough

structure that you might
suppose, but living tissue which
the doctors say a woman of my age

should nurture mindfully with fruit,
weightbearing exercise, and supplements
to halt the dangers of a fracture when I'm old;

and because I love you I will also tell
how stripped of skin the papery bone
is worthy of inscription, could hold

a detailed record of a navy or a store of grain,
and how, if it's preserved
according to the pharaohs,

wrapped in bandages of coca leaf, tobacco,
it will survive long after all our books,
and even words are weightless;

and perhaps because the heaviness of your head,
the way I love the slow, sweet sense of you,
the easiness by which you're stilled,

how the fleshy structures that your skeleton,
your skull maintain, are easily interrogated,
it reminds me how our hands,

clasped for a moment, now, amount
to everything I have; how even your smile
as it breaks me up, has the quality of ice,

the long lines of loneliness
like a lifetime ploughed across a palm,
the permanence of snow.

# My Father's Hair

For it has stood up like a coxcomb before a fight.
For it is whiter than lace on a bobbin or snow on a bough.
For in his youth it was auburn, leading to blackness.
For it has a grave insouciance,
What they call in Sassoon's "a natural air".
For it has resisted gels and lotions, brilliantine, mousses.
For it has been photographed, ridiculed,
Admired, swept back.
For it speaks the language of wild things, everywhere.
For it has suffered the barbary of barbers, and my mother.
For it has been tamed with deerstalkers,
Baseball and camouflage caps.
For it is something of a pirate or an admiral.
It is a spark transmitter and a Special Constable,
It is Harrier, Jumpjet, parachute, Chinook.
For it is salt on an eyelash, fresh from the sea.
For it is loved by many women of the district,
And is piped aboard the sternest of vessels.
For it cannot be mentioned, the pot of *Vitalis*
She gave him on their honeymoon.
For its mind is as fast as light, the elastic stretch
Of a falling star. It is not anybody's servant.
For we will say nothing of Delilah and Seville.
It is both gravel path and skating rink.
It is velvet, it is epaulettes. It is sunrise, it is sunset.
O my father's hair! It is an unsung hero!
But because of the sickness, or the cure for the sickness,
It lies like an angel's on the pillow:
Long white strands, like wings, or long white wings, like hair.

# Atlantis

*for my parents*

I try to imagine you dead,
caught now in this moment of love
as if trapped spectacularly in a lava flow
and sunk beneath the waves —
just now, as you hold each other,
arm resting on waist or thigh,
lip breathing on lip;

and I try to imagine myself,
grown suddenly old
at the point of your dying,
at this moment when I see
how love begins,
becomes itself again;
and when that tenderness

again becomes desire
so that your children's children's
children, in a look, a word, perhaps,
an errant vowel, might find you,
somehow, by mistake
an ice-blue underwater city

suddenly come across.

# The Oral Tradition

*"So ends this branch...."*

Twinned from the start, suckled by the same wolf,
except we were two foreign cities: familiar as our own
four hands, and yet the more we looked the stranger —
you were my more-ish funny little man, mustachio-ed,
like Gorky, and I your *streetwise cookie*, broken-hearted lass,
ironic and kind-eyed, the bird-in-the-hand
when the bird had flown: *Deryn aderyn bach....*
    I'll remember your words that first time, *That's enough*
our *paned o de / cupán té* exchange,
and trips in the *glúaisteán*, our easy motorings as,
your braided charioteer, your *kore*, I drove us to the Underworld
of Peckham, Nunhead, Dog Kennel Hill,
no Cerberus at our wingèd heels, but flaky pastries
in our hands, and cornflowers, medallions
of bright cheese, and blackberries, and newspapers
and pots of homemade jam....
    I'll remember, too, the chequered sofa where we'd loll,
undoing the rigging so I'd sail you home, and *slippery blisses*,
your stubborn streak, your womanly look when stripped to
                        the waist
and pegging out the washing, the hedgehog with her
                        snuffling gait,
the jasmine bower, tornado talk, our mouth-to-
mouth, our cheek-to-cheek; the words that gave us pleasure
even then: mongoose, lugubrious, *con brio*... the way you'd
                        sleep —
knee bent, arms stretched, in a position of recovery:
*Don't come anywhere near my mouth, sweetheart....*
And waspy pints across the Rye, dreaming of shorts
forever; Elizabeth, from the interior, and Cal, and John;
and Huffy Henry on his best behaviour,
and fish and túrmeric, papríka! *What wonders* was *she sitting on* ?
and Magnus Martyr where we wrote our names,
*splendour of white and gold....*

But because I believe in an elegy, not only to the dead,
not only to loss, and because we, in spite of it all, came through
and live, testament to the awkwardness
of human nature, love-gone-wrong, the old tricks
of the persistent gods; and because I believe, too, in the human
-ness of our ineptitude, bad timing, the fickleness
of love, but also in its celebration
this is a lover's gift, a prayer to the living
and the love we give away....

For now we've learned
to think both gratefully and kindly, of your children and my
                                        future children,
friends come home to each other, if you like, able to tell each
                                                        other
all our truths, both holy and unholy, strange and sore,
know that I keep a special store — of Guinness, and *porcini*,
Feverfew, and Selfheal, Forget-Me-Not to anoint your garden,
in honour too, of private griefs we've shared; that tonight
it's for the love of friendship and our love
when I look up at the cold sky, see what I saw, years back,
when you whispered constellations; and know
that this telling of our history's not nostalgia, but
a placing of ourselves in time, two specks of dust
on the earth's circumference, two compasses encompassing
                                        the years.
        So I whisper the stars back to you, over the roofs
of Liverpool and London, a twinkle in the eye; Venus,
                                        winking there,
behind the clouds, Sirius the Dog Star, Ursa Major
and her progeny... *Le ghrá, cariad,* the whole bright universe
                                        beyond.

# Spells

## (i)

The bed becomes a page, the white sheets
where we leave ourselves,
hair, fluids, sloughed off skin,
cells of the self grown out of themselves
not living but unchanged, as any lover's history.
And here, like a wing, or a sycamore seed
is the L of my arm, and here is my hand
on your halo of hair. I want to spell out all
the harboured messages of joy, make an alphabet
of our hands and bodies, rewrite our movements,
make everything strange. To speak what is us,
what is you, or me: each vowel, each consonant,
now coded in the silent movements of our sleep.

## (ii)

The vowels, the consonants of speech, sound wrong
because like all translators we have failed. We learn to misread
or adequately speak, the words that waltz, cavort or slip,
terrible on the starry page. Instead, we're left with all the painful
ghostings of ourselves. *Her voice* in another language, the way
you say
*His eyes.* And words as unaccountable to things as love.
And memories slither. And thoughts collide.
When we dream it is ice that we dream of, and snow.
When you say that you love me, you say it in sleep.
*We're all of us dying, but I want this to live.*
Our days collapse, the nights draw in. A smudge of mouth,
a flurry of hands. Even the darkness is crying out
Through the pale O of your dreaming mouth.

(iii)

Your soft mouth says my name,
makes me unfamiliar, makes me look at myself
from a distance again. But
the soft V of my breasts that I find
when at last you take hold of me, puts me to flight.
And this flight's still a bird's, or an echo of bird
as softly I push into you, feathering your eyelids
with my tongue, strobing a cool sandpapery cheek.
And when I write of myself,
it is now as a 2, our joined lives
make the shape of a swan. *What makes us afraid?*
Beside us in the emerald water
the swan's white reflection.

(iv)

Your long body is a history I want to find a way to read
negotiating bends and swan-like corners,
the map of constellations on your back, the isthmus
of your ankle, the wayward hill of your contoured chest,
peaks of your buttocks, lovely knees.
I try to read you backwards, frontways,
from top to bottom, right to left. I whisper in morse
to colour your dreams, then signal my errors,
eight semaphore Es. And if love is a mirror I see only your face.
And if love is a window I tap at the glass. If I licked you alive,
would the whole summer warm me? My sighs are spells,
they are gasps for breath. The question-mark of your loving body
rousing me at last to speech.

# Natural Selection

*'Sit, then, and talk with her. She is thine own'*
*The Tempest*

So this is where the brides come with their mates —
Emerging from the undergrowth that's
Noted for its fauna and its flora:
An extravagance of bluetits, yellowhammers, finches,
The bosky acres and the unshrubbed down, the peonies,
The daisies and forget-me-nots grown wild,
An ordinariness of nature grown fabulously strange....
And then these women in their antiquated gowns,
Bedecked, bejewelled, their empire necklines, and tiaras,
In lemons, mauves, and olive-ochres,
Their nets, their silks, their magically floating trains,
Who pose, confettied, on an arch-browed bridge, beside a tree,
Their husbands, nervous, and cravatted —
Alert as unbacked colts, almost extinguished by the heat
Laughing, or solemn now, by turn,
In their curious stripes, in their tails....
The photographer with a dog-fish face, a tripod, camera, smiles,
Moving them together in a freeze-frame dance
That will tell of the moment, or the rehearsal of a moment:
*Honours, riches, marriage-blessing!*
A dark-haired groom, a bright-eyed bride....
And still I do not know what scene it is I'm entering
As bullfrogs lollop gracelessly into the lake,
Like the moments of love, themselves,
In an amphibious transition — around them, all the burry sounds
Of nature busy going wild. I feel the sun on my face,
And smile and watch, in jeans and trainers and my oldest shirt,
As they stand before me, pair upon pair:
Groom, bride, bride, groom, groom, bride....
And how do we decide? On the best ways to love,
The dearest, the safest? On the kindest or the necessary,
Or the true? What ceremonies fit
A need for permanence, and who am I to ask,
Interrogate the need for such commemoration of desire —
A wish, a silent prayer for growth, the permanence

Of change? Or the integrity of love itself, the chance to make
A monkey or an angel of ourselves; for something
That has goodness at its heart? Here, amongst the leaves,
The weeping willows on the short-grassed green,
The rhapsodies, the heat, the becoming and the unbecoming lives?

Nagyerdei Park, Debrecen,
September 1997

# The Policeman's Daughter

*after Paula Rego*

When I see her there, shining her daddy's boots, the moonlight
                                    making the sky a deep
Improper blue,
I want to fill the night with stars, with rain;

I want for there to be a kind of stillness that as yet she can't
                                    contain:
Between the silent walls, this kitten's mew
And all the strange geometries of sleep

That in her task she will refuse.... O to heap
Words on her! Flowers! Suitors! Anything to
Take away the look of studied pain;

To unravel that moonsoaked mane,
To make her someone ordinary who
Suffers for a while; who doesn't keep

Her father wedged so deep
Against her heart she hasn't anything but this to do:
To scrub and polish, rub and spit — each night at it again —

As if this making of her hand a hoof, making the leather strain
Against her fingers, *so,*
Would always be enough, would heap

Like a backwards prayer, scorn on her enemies, keep
Sweet the properties of life; make something new
From nothing — the point where land meets sky

And's not itself or anything:
Which is like love, where we begin.

# Acknowledgements

Thanks to the editors of the journals and anthologies in which some of these poems, in various versions, first appeared: *Critical Survey, London Magazine, New Welsh Review, Poetry Canada, Poetry Review, Poetry Wales, Verse,* and *Liverpool Accents: Seven Poets and a City,* ed. Peter Robinson.

I would also like to thank the Arts Council of England for a Writer's Award in 1996.

Thanks of a very different sort to Maurice Riordan, Matt Simpson, Alison Mark, Sally Kilmister, Gwyneth Lewis, Tom Lynch and Amy Wack; but especially to Michael Murphy, who in all sorts of ways has helped see this book through.